THE EXTRAORDINARY ADVENTURES OF

MR BENN

RED KNIGHT

Based on the TV series by David McKee

Hodder
Children's
Books

A division of Hodder Children's Books

Red Knight, Caveman, Diver and Spaceman
First published in 1993
This edition published in 2009

Text copyright © David McKee 1993
Illustrations copyright © King Rollo Films Ltd 1993

Hodder Children's Books, 338 Euston Road, London, NW1 3BH
Hodder Children's Books Australia, Level 17/207 Kent Street, Sydney, NSW 2000

ISBN: 978 0 340 99715 4

Printed in China

Hodder Children's Books is a division of Hachette Children's Books.
An Hachette UK Company.

www.hachette.co.uk

It was Saturday morning in Festive Road. Men were unloading their vans, boys were playing with wooden swords. Everything was ordinary.
At number 52 the postman arrived with a letter for Mr Benn. It was an invitation to a fancy dress party.

Mr Benn wasn't very fond of parties but he did like
fancy dress, so off he went in search of something
special to wear.

He tried the big shops, but he didn't find anything.
He tried the not-so-big shops. He tried the small
shops. But he couldn't find fancy dress anywhere,
only ordinary, everyday clothes.

At last, in a back lane, he found a little shop with all sorts of interesting things to wear. In the window was a suit of bright red armour.

"Just the ticket," thought Mr Benn, so in he went.

As if by magic, the shopkeeper appeared. "Can I help you, sir?" he asked.

"I wonder if I might borrow that suit of red armour?"

"Of course," replied the shopkeeper. "Try it on," and he pointed to the changing room.

Quickly Mr Benn put on the armour. He laughed at the red knight reflected in the mirror. Then he noticed another door.

"Well I never," he said, and he walked through the second doorway.

On the other side, Mr Benn found himself in rocky countryside. He looked around and spotted smoke rising from behind a large pile of rocks. He felt brave in his red armour, so he climbed up the rocks to see what was making the smoke.

Down below, he saw a large dragon breathing out clouds of smoke.

"It's someone else in fancy dress," he thought. So he called down, "That's a good outfit. How do you make the smoke?"

"You can't fool me," said the dragon. "You've been sent to kill me."

"Kill him?" thought Mr Benn. "He really is a dragon, but a very sad dragon."

Before long, Mr Benn was sitting down beside the dragon, and the dragon told him his story.

He used to live happily in a castle. He worked hard lighting all the fires. But, one day, a man came with a new idea for lighting fires: he had matches. Now nobody wanted matches because they liked the dragon to light their fires. The matchmaker was cross about this so he set fire to a barn or two and blamed the dragon.

When the king's favourite white horse ran away, the dragon was told it was his fault too. The poor dragon couldn't do anything right and was sent away from the castle in shame. Now everyone had to buy the matchmaker's matches.

The dragon looked crestfallen and pointed to the horse.
"I've been looking after him, but I'm much too afraid to return him."

"I'll help you," said Mr Benn. "Show me where the castle is and I'll tell the king the true story."

The dragon was delighted, and they set off for the castle straight away.

They walked and walked, but the nearer they got, the slower the
dragon went. Then, when they saw the castle in the distance, the
dragon stopped completely.

"I'll just wait here under the trees until you return," he said.

Seeing how nervous the dragon was, Mr Benn said goodbye, and rode off towards the castle on the fine white horse.

When the guards saw
Mr Benn, they rushed to
tell the king that the dragon
must have been killed because
a brave red knight was riding
up to the castle on his white
horse. They took him straight
to the king for his reward.

The king listened while Mr Benn told him the dragon's sad story. The king was so happy because he had missed the dragon and was delighted to hear the truth. Nobody liked the nasty matchmaker. He had been cheating the people by making his matches more and more expensive.

"Bring the matchmaker here," said the king.

The people booed and hissed as the miserable matchmaker was brought before him.

"I order you to go to prison," he thundered, and the guards took him to the deepest, darkest dungeon, while the king decided how to punish the rascal.

"Now take me to the dragon," said the king. Mr Benn led the king and his guards to welcome back the dragon.

Just before they reached the dragon's hiding place, the procession stopped because they didn't want to frighten him. The king and Mr Benn got off their horses and walked to the trees where the dragon was crouching.

The king was happy to see the dragon again, and told him how sorry he was for all his troubles.

The dragon was so overjoyed that he made the king and Mr Benn ride on his back.

With the dragon leading the way in triumph and the guards following behind cheering, they made their way back to the castle.

Everybody came to welcome the dragon.
The king made a speech and explained how
the matchmaker was the troublemaker, not the
dragon. As punishment, the matchmaker would
have to make as many matches as the people
needed for nothing. From now on, the dragon
would be the king's personal firelighter.
Everyone cheered and clapped.

Then the king thanked Mr Benn and said that to celebrate there would be a magnificent feast, and Mr Benn would be the guest of honour.

Preparations started, and everyone set to,
to make it the finest feast ever.

While everyone was rushing to and fro,
with puddings and cakes, pies and tureens,
Mr Benn stood at the side and watched.

Suddenly a familiar little man appeared.

"Would you like to change before the feast, sir?" he asked. "You'll find the other clothes in here." And he showed Mr Benn through a door... into the changing room of the shop!

Mr Benn took a last look at himself in the mirror. Slowly he took off the helmet, the gloves and the fine suit of red armour, and put on his usual clothes.

"I've had too much excitement for one day to go to the fancy dress party now," said Mr Benn. "I won't take it after all."

"Right you are, sir," smiled the little man. "Shall we be seeing you again?"

"Oh yes," said Mr Benn. "I'll be back very soon."

Mr Benn walked home. As he put his hand into his pocket for his keys, he found a very unusual box of matches. He smiled at the picture on the box.

"How nice," he thought. "I'll keep it, just to remind me."

THE EXTRAORDINARY ADVENTURES OF

MR BENN

CAVEMAN

Based on the TV series by David McKee

Hodder
Children's
Books

A division of Hodder Children's Books

Festive Road was usually very quiet but on this morning,
the street was crowded with traffic. At number 52
Mr Benn looked out of his window.

"What's going on?" he asked a man.

"The main road is being repaired and it's the rush hour," said the man. "All the traffic has to come this way."

Mr Benn walked back inside and sat down to look at the television. He watched a film about cavemen. It said that cavemen lived a long time ago in caves. They dressed in furs and worked with tools made out of stone. Mr Benn was very interested, but the traffic outside was so noisy that he couldn't really hear the television.

"I must get away from all this noise," he said, and he thought about the special costume shop that he knew, the shop where adventures could start. "That's the place to go," he smiled.

Mr Benn was soon in the lane with the shop. He paused for a moment outside, then went in. He looked at the costumes.

"Something away from cars," he thought.

As if by magic the shopkeeper appeared. "Good morning, sir," he said.

"Good morning," said Mr Benn. "Is this a caveman's outfit?"

"Yes," said the shopkeeper. "They used to live in caves, you know."

"They didn't have any cars either," said Mr Benn. "Do you think I might try it on?"

He took the costume into the changing room and quickly changed. He smiled at the furry Mr Benn in the mirror and then went through the door that could lead to an adventure.

On the other side of the door everything was very dark. Mr Benn could see a light ahead and walked towards it. As it became lighter, he found himself walking out of a cave. In front of him were other caves and lots of people dressed in furs.

Mr Benn went over to a patch of grass and lay down. He closed his eyes and thought how peaceful it was. The sun was shining.

"I wonder why the cave people don't lie out here. It's lovely," he thought. It wasn't long before he knew why.

From a long way off came a rumbling noise. At the same time, the cave people started to shout. In the distance was a great cloud of dust coming closer and closer.

The cavemen were shouting, "Look out!" and "Get out of the way!" and "Run for it!"

Mr Benn jumped to his feet and raced back to the caves just as a huge animal thundered past.

"Golly!" said Mr Benn. "What was that?"

"A dinosaur," said a man. "Every morning the dinosaurs rush past here on their way to get to the best feeding places. And every evening they race back to get the best places to sleep."

Suddenly there was a crash and the dinosaurs screeched to a halt. Some of them had fallen over, blocking the road.

"That's always happening," said the man. "They're so impatient, no manners at all."

And with that the dinosaurs picked themselves up and rushed off again.

The cave people settled down to their supper.

Mr Benn asked, "Why do you stay here? There must be other places to live away from the dinosaurs."

"Not with caves," said the man. "And we need caves to live in."

When the meal was over, Mr Benn settled down under a pile of furs for the night.

The next morning when Mr Benn woke up, he saw some men trying to move a dinosaur. "Can I help?" he asked.

"This often happens," explained a man. "An animal just parks here to sleep and blocks the entrance of a cave. Help us push it out of the way, will you?"

So Mr Benn got behind the dinosaur and they pushed and heaved it out of the way.

When Mr Benn was having his breakfast, he heard the rumbling noise again and sure enough, the animals went rushing past – this time in the opposite direction.

When all the dinosaurs had gone, Mr Benn asked if he could go for a walk to get away from the dust.

"Yes, we'll all go," said the others. "You have to be careful crossing the dinosaur road. The dinosaurs don't mean any harm but if one does bump into you, it can be quite nasty."

They looked first one way, then the other. A large cloud of dust was approaching. They waited until the dinosaur had passed. This time when they looked the road was clear, so they crossed. But they kept looking each way in case a dinosaur should suddenly appear. But none did.

As they walked on, the countryside became greener. There were trees and streams, and the air was fresh. The children played freely and everyone was much happier.

"This is where we would really like to live," said one of the men.

"Why don't you?" asked Mr Benn.

"Because there are no caves, silly," the man laughed.

"Build some, or at least something that will do instead," said Mr Benn.
"I'll show you how to build huts with these stones."

Mr Benn showed them how to place the stones one
on top of the other. As soon as the cave people saw
how it was done, they started to build several huts.

When the walls were finished, Mr Benn took them into the woods to get some branches for the roofs. Next they cut pieces of turf from the ground, then they laid the turf on the branches.

Lo and behold, the huts were complete!
The people were very pleased.

"From now on we can live here," they agreed.

A man appeared beside Mr Benn.
"Come and look inside this hut, sir," he said.

Just then, Mr Benn heard a noise in the distance. The cave people were standing on top of a hill. They were watching the dinosaurs' rush hour again. After the dinosaurs had gone, Mr Benn went into the hut and, just as he had expected, he found himself back in the changing room of the shop.

Mr Benn returned the outfit to the shopkeeper and said, "Thank you very much."

"Thank you, sir," said the shopkeeper. "We look forward to seeing you again."

As Mr Benn waved goodbye from the door he said, "I look forward to seeing you again too."

Mr Benn walked back along Festive Road which
was still filled with cars and lorries.

"Somehow they seem different now," thought Mr Benn, and for a moment he imagined that they looked like dinosaurs.

At his gate Mr Benn realised that he was holding
something in his hand. It was a stone hammer.

"I wonder how long I've been holding that," he thought.
"I'll keep it. It's just what I need to help me remember."

THE EXTRAORDINARY ADVENTURES OF

MR BENN

DIVER

Based on the TV series by David McKee

Hodder
Children's
Books

A division of Hodder Children's Books

In Festive Road people were going about their business as usual, and children were playing with their holiday seashells, listening to the sound of the sea.

Number 52 is Mr Benn's house, but there was no sign of Mr Benn.

He wasn't in his room. He wasn't in his garden.
And he wasn't in the park.

Mr Benn was by the river, looking at the boats and
thinking about the adventures they have. "It's time
I had a new adventure. I'll pay a visit to that special
costume shop." And off he went.

Inside the shop, as if by magic, the shopkeeper appeared.
"Good morning, sir," he said. "What would you like to try today?"

"Is that a frogman's underwater outfit?" asked Mr Benn.

"Yes," replied the shopkeeper. "Try it on."

Mr Benn went into the changing room and quickly put on the frogman's outfit and the special breathing tube so he could swim underwater.

"Now for the door that leads to a new adventure," he said.

On the other side of the door, Mr Benn found himself among rocks beside the sea. He walked to the water's edge and got ready to jump in.

"Hey! Mind out!" shouted some sailors on a red boat.

"It's an underwater boat," thought Mr Benn. "It's a submarine."

"We're going to look for a monster," shouted the captain. "If you see the green submarine, you can say that we'll see the monster first." And the crew climbed into the submarine and it slowly slid into the water.

Mr Benn was about to jump into the water when there was another shout. "Hey! Mind out!"

This time Mr Benn saw a green submarine.

"We're going to look for the monster," shouted the captain. "If you see the red submarine, you can say that we'll see it first. Look out! We're going to dive."

And the green submarine slowly slid into the water too.

Mr Benn walked along the shore and met an old sailor who said, "Hello, are you looking for the monster as well?"

"No, I'm not looking for the monster," said Mr Benn, "but tell me about it."

"People say there is a monster living in the waters around here," smiled the old sailor. "These two submarines are racing to see who will be the first to photograph it, and they won't stop until there is a winner."

"Well, I'm looking for an adventure," said Mr Benn, and with that he jumped into the water.

Beneath the surface it was like being in a different world. Mr Benn was happy to swim around just looking at the fish. He had quite forgotten about the submarines until he saw the red one gliding past him. A little later the green one went past.

"Those submarines are a nuisance," he thought,
so he swam to the bottom of the sea.

Just when he thought he had seen everything, he spotted a mermaid sitting on a rock and holding something to her ear.

"Hello," he said, "you're the first mermaid I've ever seen. But surely you can hear the sea without listening to it in a shell?"

"It's not the sea I'm listening to," she said. "You listen."

Mr Benn put the shell to his ear. "It sounds like the wind," he said at last.

"Yes," said the mermaid, "but I'm looking for a new shell for King Neptune's birthday, and he already has one that makes that sound."

"Do you mean to say that you can hear different sounds in different shells?" asked Mr Benn.

"Oh yes," said the mermaid. "King Neptune has shells with the sound of the wind, the rain, birds – all sorts of things."

"I'll help you search for a new one," said Mr Benn. But every shell he found, it seemed that King Neptune already had. Then he picked up an unusual shell that sounded like the buzzing of a bee.

"He certainly doesn't have that one," said the mermaid. "Come with me and bring it to King Neptune."

They swam and swam and came to King Neptune's cave.

"Happy Birthday," they said, giving him the new shell. King Neptune was delighted.

Beside the king sat a huge animal. "Is that the monster the submarines are looking for?" asked Mr Benn.

"Yes, it's my pet monster," said the king. "Those submarines frighten him. I do wish they'd leave us in peace."

"Can't you ask the submarines to go away?" pleaded the mermaid. "It's not a very nice birthday for King Neptune."

"They are having a race to photograph the monster, but I have an idea," said Mr Benn. And he swam back to the shore.

There he soon found the green submarine.
"Have you seen the monster yet?" he asked
the captain.

"No," growled the captain.

"You've probably frightened it away," said Mr Benn. "If you
dressed up your submarine to look like another monster, it
wouldn't be frightened. Then you could get close enough to
photograph it."

"That's a grand idea," said the captain, and told the crew to make a monster costume to cover the submarine.

Then Mr Benn went to the red submarine and said exactly the same thing to the other captain.

With that, Mr Benn swam quickly back to King Neptune's cave.

"I've played a little trick on the two submarines," he said. "Let's see if it works. Follow me." Mr Benn led the way and they hid behind a huge pile of rocks. "Now watch."

In the distance they could see a monster. "That's really the red submarine in a monster's outfit," said Mr Benn. "And that's the green submarine," he chuckled as another monster appeared.

The two submarine monsters moved round taking photographs of each other. They both thought they'd got a photograph of the monster.

"We've won," cheered the red submarine.

"We've won," cheered the green submarine.

And away they sailed.

King Neptune was delighted, and the real monster gave Mr Benn a ride back to the shore.

At the water's edge, Mr Benn waved goodbye to the king and the mermaid. Then he looked round for the submarines.

Sure enough, they soon sailed past. The captain of the red submarine smiled and waved a photograph of a huge monster. The captain of the green submarine smiled and waved a photograph of another huge monster.

"Well, they both have their photographs," said the shopkeeper, who had suddenly appeared beside him. "You deserve a rest. Come into this cave and sit down."

Mr Benn walked into the cave and, just as he had expected, he found himself back in the changing room. He put his own clothes on and handed over the underwater outfit.

"Look, there's a seashell stuck to the suit," smiled the shopkeeper.

"It will make a good souvenir," said Mr Benn.

Back at his house in Festive Road, Mr Benn listened to the seashell. He wasn't sure if it was the sea he could hear or the wind.

"Anyway," he said, "it's just the thing to help me remember."

THE EXTRAORDINARY ADVENTURES OF

MR BENN

SPACEMAN

Based on the TV series by David McKee

Hodder
Children's
Books

A division of Hodder Children's Books

It was just an ordinary day in Festive Road.
Boys played with toy rockets while their mothers
brought home the shopping.

Number 52 was Mr Benn's house
but he was nowhere to be seen.

Mr Benn was in the back garden talking to his neighbour.

"Why is it," asked the neighbour, "that your grass looks greener than mine?"

"That's strange," said Mr Benn, "I always think yours looks greener than mine." And they both laughed.

Mr Benn decided to go for a walk in the park.
He sat on a bench and watched a boy flying a kite.

"I wonder if it would go above the clouds if the string
was long enough," he thought. "It would be so
interesting to go up above the clouds."

All of a sudden Mr Benn tingled with excitement
as he remembered the costume shop.

In almost no time at all, Mr Benn was in the special shop where adventures start. As if by magic, the shopkeeper appeared.

"Good morning, sir. I do believe you've made up your mind already."

"I'd like to try the space outfit," said Mr Benn.

"You know the way, sir," replied the shopkeeper, pointing to the changing room.

Mr Benn changed into the space outfit. He looked at himself in the mirror and then headed for the door that always led to adventures.

On the other side he found himself in a spaceship.
Another spaceman was at the controls.

"Hello," he said, "ready for the blast off? Here we go then."

Mr Benn felt the spaceship surge as it lifted off.

"Where are we going?" said Mr Benn as he watched the stars through the window.

"To a planet covered with gold and jewels. We'll be rich," said the spaceman.

"That would be fun," thought Mr Benn. But all he could see was a very ordinary planet.

The spaceship landed with a bump. Lying all around were lumps of glittering gold and jewels, just as the spaceman had said.

"We're rich!" said the spaceman. And they walked around picking up the best jewels and pieces of gold they could find.

All of a sudden they met a man dressed in rags, sitting on a lump of gold.

"Hello," said the man. "What are you going to do with that load?"

The spaceman laughed, "We're rich. We can do anything we like."

"I'm afraid you're wrong," said the ragged man. "It's no good to you at all. There are no shops on this planet so there's nowhere to spend the riches. Anyway, as soon as you leave this planet they turn into ordinary stones. The next planet is the place to be. There they live in comfort and everything is free."

"In that case, we may as well go to the next planet," said the spaceman.
So they put down their gold and jewels and made their way back to
the spaceship.

But Mr Benn took one piece of gold with him to see what it would look
like when it changed to stone.

The spaceship zoomed away from the planet on its journey.

"There it is," said the spaceman, as they spotted another planet coming very close.

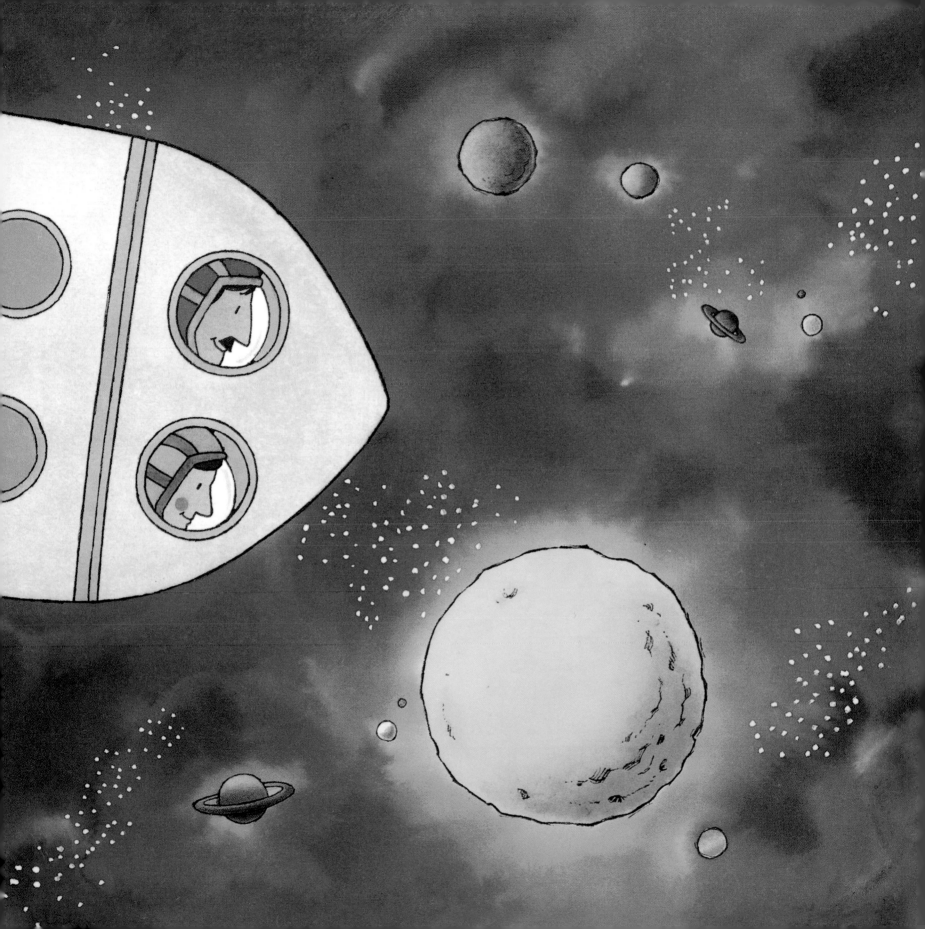

The spaceship landed near a town. Mr Benn and the spaceman saw that the shops were full of things, and nobody looked poor. At restaurants people sat outside and ate for free. Mr Benn and the spaceman sat down too. But something was wrong. They noticed that apart from themselves everything looked colourless.

"Tell us about this dullness," they said to the waiter.

"Well," he said, "there's no colour here at all, and if you stay here very long, you'll be just like us. But there is another planet not far away where everything is very bright."

"That's for us," said the spaceman. "Let's go there. I don't fancy a life without colour."

Back in the spaceship, Mr Benn watched the grey planet getting smaller and smaller as they headed towards the next planet.

"I hope the next planet really will be better," said Mr Benn as they flew nearer.

"We'll have a good look round first," replied the spaceman. "And we won't get out if we see anything wrong."

Once they had landed, they peered out of the windows. Everything looked all right. Colourful birds flew past. There were bright flowers and trees. They saw gaily coloured houses. People dressed in vivid clothes were walking about.

Mr Benn and the spaceman looked through the telescopes just to make sure. The only unusual thing they could see was the hats that everyone wore pulled down over their ears.

"Just the fashion," said the spaceman. "Let's go outside."

But they soon realised that the hats were not just fashion.
Everyone had their ears covered for one very good reason:
the air was filled with the most horrible screeching noises.

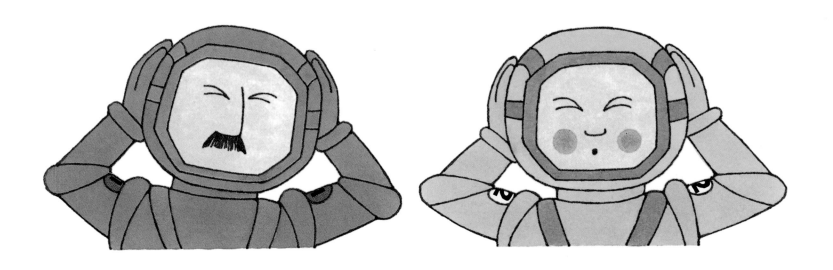

Mr Benn and the spaceman ran back to the spaceship and took off into the night. Before they had gone far, the spaceman said, "I'm lost. We'll have to stop at the next planet we pass and ask the way."

So once again they landed. This time the planet was very hot, too hot in fact, but at least it was quiet. Nobody was about. Then, as if by magic, a man appeared. It was the shopkeeper.

"We're lost," explained the spaceman. "We've been to all sorts of planets but we don't know where to go next."

"There is a place that is not altogether perfect, but then there is not much wrong with it either," said the shopkeeper.

"We'll try there," said the spaceman.

"I think I'll stay here," said Mr Benn. "I've had enough of travelling."

"It's very hot, sir," said the shopkeeper. "Step into the cave and keep cool."

Mr Benn went into the cave and, as he expected, he was back in the changing room of the shop. He changed into his own clothes.

"Where did you send the spaceman?" he asked as he returned the spaceman outfit.

"Here, sir, back to Earth," said the shopkeeper. "It's not perfect, but it's not too bad either."

Back in Festive Road, people went about their business as usual.
At his gate, Mr Benn took the lump of stone out of his pocket.

"Nobody would believe that this was once gold," he thought.
"But I'll always keep it. Then I will remember."